Jobs if You Like...

Science

Charlotte Guillain

Heinemann
LIBRARY
Chicago, Illinois

www.capstonepub.com
Visit our website to find out more information about Heinemann-Raintree books.

To order:

☎ Phone 800-747-4992

💻 Visit www.capstonepub.com to browse our catalog and order online.

Edited by Rebecca Rissman, Daniel Nunn, and Adrian Vigliano
Designed by Steve Mead
Picture research by Mica Brancic
Originated by Capstone Global Library
Printed and bound in China by South China Printing Company

16 15 14 13 12
10 9 8 7 6 5 4 3 2 1

Library of Congress Cataloging-in-Publication Data
Guillain, Charlotte.
  Science / Charlotte Guillain.—1st ed.
    p. cm.—(Jobs if you like...)
  Includes bibliographical references and index.
  ISBN 978-1-4329-6811-3 (hb)—ISBN 978-1-4329-6822-9 (pb) 1. Science—Vocational guidance—Juvenile literature. I. Title.
  Q147.G85 2013
  502.3—dc23   2011031931

Acknowledgments
We would like to thank the following for permission to reproduce photographs: Alamy pp. 6 (© H. Mark Weidman Photography), 25 (© Mark Conlin); Corbis pp. 24 (© Jeffrey L. Rotman), 26 (© John Madere); ESA p. 19; Getty Images pp. 12 (Stone/Arnulf Husmo), 21; Glow Images pp. 14 (Blue Jean Images), 23 (Corbis/©LWA-Stephen Welstead), 20 (Denkou Images), 17 (FotoSearch RF), 9 (Inspirestock), 16 (Johner RF/Jeppe Wikstrom), 27 (Moodboard Premium), 13 (SodaClassic/Pundurs Armands); NASA pp. 4, 11, 18; Shutterstock pp. 5, 22 (© Alexander Raths), 10 (© Anetta), 8 (© Dmitry Kalinovsky), 7 (© Konstantin Sutyagin); Superstock p. 15 (Age Fotostock/Javier Larrea).

Cover photo of scientists in the Antarctic reproduced with permission of Getty Images (National Geographic/Paul Nicklen).

Every effort has been made to contact copyright holders of material reproduced in this book. Any omissions will be rectified in subsequent printings if notice is given to the publisher.

Disclaimer
All the Internet addresses (URLs) given in this book were valid at the time of going to press. However, due to the dynamic nature of the Internet, some addresses may have changed, or sites may have changed or ceased to exist since publication. While the author and publisher regret any inconvenience this may cause readers, no responsibility for any such changes can be accepted by either the author or the publisher.

Contents

Some words are shown in bold, **like this**. You can find out what they mean by looking in the glossary.

Why Does Science Matter?

Do you learn about science at school? We need science to understand how our bodies work. We also know about outer space and the world around us because of science. Science is all about exploring and making exciting discoveries!

People couldn't explore space without science!

Scientists are making new discoveries all the time.

We need science for so many things in our lives. We don't even know what amazing things scientists will find out next! Read this book to find out about some great jobs that use science. Could one of them be for you?

Be a Doctor

People need doctors when they are ill or in emergencies. If you were a doctor, you might do **surgery** to save a **patient's** life. You might decide what medicines people need or help when babies are born.

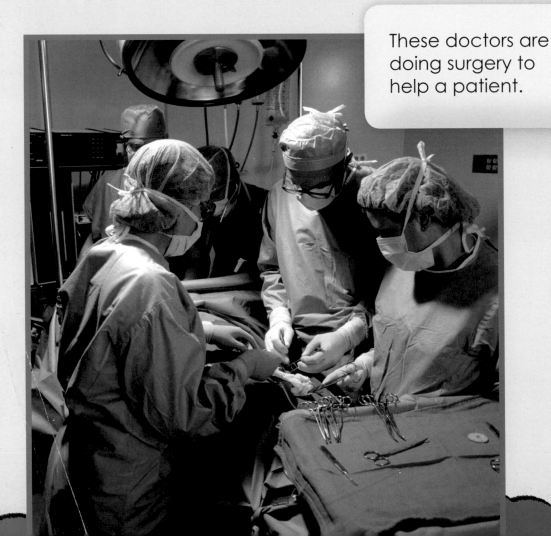

These doctors are doing surgery to help a patient.

Doctors use a lot of special **equipment** to help them do their job.

All doctors need science to do their job. They need to know how the human body works. Doctors also need to know how different **chemicals** work in drugs.

Be a Pharmacist

If people take the wrong medicine, they could be very ill. If you were a pharmacist, you could save lives by giving people the right medicines! A pharmacist can also give doctors advice on the best medicines.

Pharmacists tell people how to take different medicines.

Pharmacists need to know about the **chemicals** that are used to make medicines. They also need to understand what medicines can do to our bodies. They have to be very careful to give people the right amount of medicine.

Pharmacists need to understand science to work safely.

Be a Materials Scientist

If you like doing experiments, then maybe you could be a materials scientist. Materials scientists usually work in a **laboratory**, learning about different materials. They study what happens to **substances** when you mix, heat, or change them in other ways.

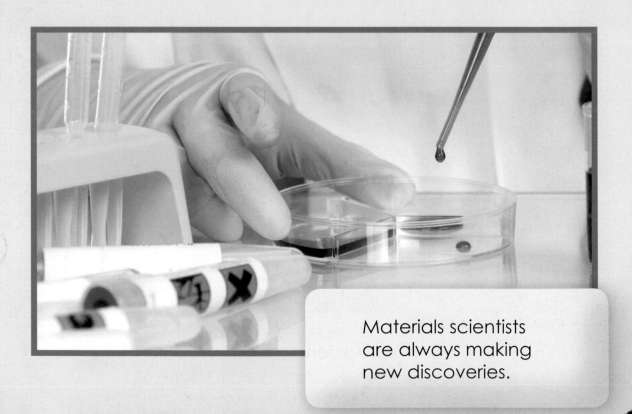

Materials scientists are always making new discoveries.

Materials scientists help to make toys, clothes, and even spacecrafts! They use science every day as they work with **chemicals** and do experiments. They need to know how to work with dangerous substances!

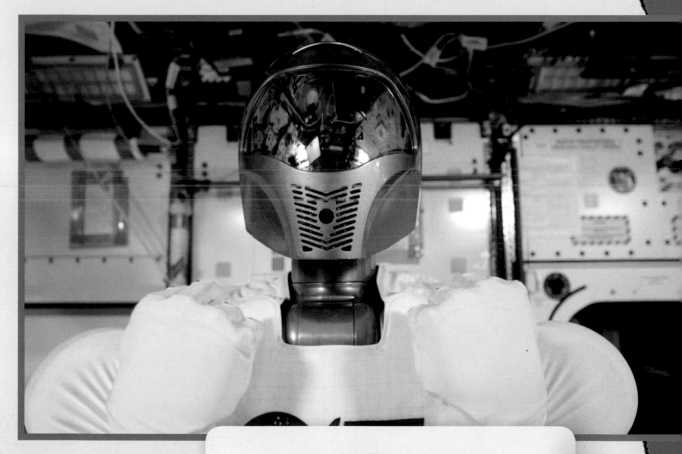

Materials scientists found the best materials to make this robot that helps astronauts.

Be an Environmental Scientist

If you were an environmental scientist, you could help protect the planet! Some environmental scientists teach people how to take care of the world. Others do **research** to find out how people affect the environment.

These environmental scientists are working in the ocean.

Many environmental scientists study plants and what they need to grow well.

Environmental scientists need science to understand the natural world. They need to know how **chemicals** can cause problems in nature. They also know what plants and animals need to be healthy.

Be a Food Scientist

If you were a food scientist, you would make sure the food we eat is safe. You could also make some food taste better! Sometimes food scientists make food look nicer or last longer.

Food scientists look at different ways to grow food.

Some food scientists have to taste food to check that it tastes right.

Food scientists need science to understand which food is good for us. They also need to know what **chemicals** are safe to use when we make food. They might use science to make food healthier for us to eat.

Be a Pilot

If you were a pilot, you would use science to fly. You might carry passengers from place to place or fly fighter jets in the military. Some helicopter pilots rush to rescue people in trouble.

Helicopter rescue pilots have to fly very carefully when they are rescuing someone.

Fighter pilots need science to do their job properly.

Pilots can't afford to make any mistakes when they are flying. They need science to understand how aircraft fly. They also need to understand how the weather can affect flying.

Be an Astronaut

Do you want a job that's out of this world? If you were an astronaut, science would take you into outer space. You could be a spacecraft pilot or build and fix **equipment**. Other astronauts do experiments to learn more about outer space.

Astronauts work together on many different science projects while they are in space.

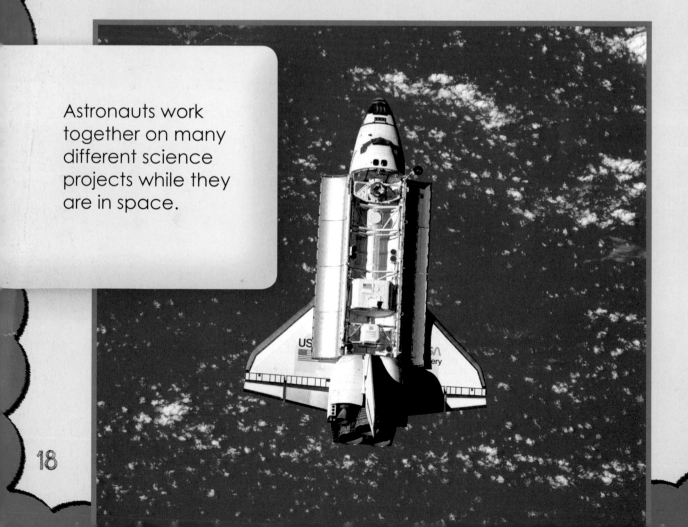

Science explains why people float in the air in space.

Astronauts need science for many different reasons. They need to study **physics** to learn about outer space. They need to understand how their bodies might change while they are in space.

Be a Sports Scientist

If you think science and sports don't mix, then think again! If you were a sports scientist, you could help people play sports better or become healthier. Some sports scientists help to make new sports **equipment**.

Some sports scientists help people to get fit again after an illness.

Some sports scientists help athletes as they train their bodies.

It is important for sports scientists to know how people's bodies work. They need to understand how hard an athlete can train without hurting his or her body. They also know which foods are best for fitness.

Be a Laboratory Technician

If you were a **laboratory** technician, you would work behind the scenes to save lives! Your experiments could find out why people are ill. You might work with other scientists to find out how to make new inventions.

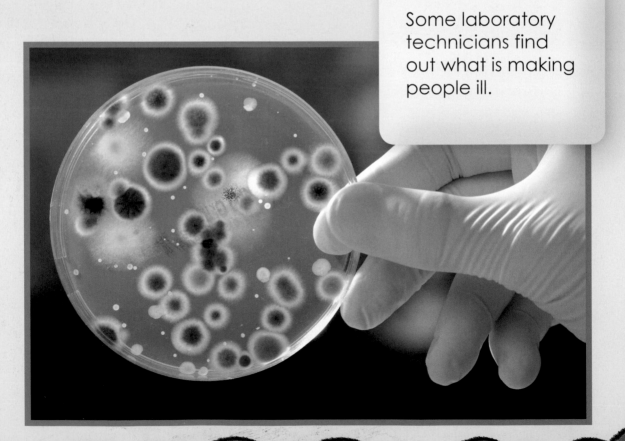

Some laboratory technicians find out what is making people ill.

Laboratory technicians need to study science so that they can do experiments properly. They need to **record** and understand information. They need to be great at solving problems.

Laboratory technicians enjoy doing experiments and finding out answers to scientific questions.

Be a Marine Biologist

If you were a marine biologist, you would learn about life in the oceans. You could study fish or other ocean animals. Or you might learn about the water in the ocean and whether it is changing due to **global warming**.

This marine biologist is studying sharks.

Some marine biologists need science to understand animals and plants. Others do experiments on seawater to see if it is getting warmer or **polluted**. They can work on and around the ocean as well as in a **laboratory**.

This marine biologist is learning about how turtles live.

Choosing the Right Job for You

When you decide what you want to do when you grow up, don't just think about school subjects. Think about what you enjoy doing. If you don't like trying new food, then don't be a food scientist!

If you enjoy traveling, then you might like to be a pilot. There are so many exciting jobs in science that there is something to suit everyone.

Five things you couldn't do without science

- Turn on a light switch
- Use a microwave oven
- Get medicine when you are ill
- Travel by plane
- Watch television

Science Job Chart

If you want to find out more about any of the jobs in this book, start here:

	Astronaut	Materials scientist	Doctor	Environmental scientist	
You need to:	Be a good team worker	Be curious	Be good with people	Care about nature	
Best thing about it:	Looking at Earth from space!	Cool experiments!	Saving lives!	Helping animals!	

Food scientist	Laboratory technician	Marine biologist	Pharmacist	Pilot	Sports scientist
Enjoy eating	Like working alone	Love the outdoors	Have a good memory	Stay calm and focused	Enjoy sports
Tasting food!	Solving problems!	Exploring the oceans!	Helping people get better!	Flying solo!	Helping athletes win!

Glossary

chemical substance made by a scientific process

equipment something made to be used in a special way

global warming warming of Earth's temperature caused by human activity

laboratory place where scientists do experiments

patient person who is ill

physics science that studies forces, light, heat, and sound, among other things

polluted made dirty or unhealthy

record write down

research find as much information about something as possible

substance type of matter or stuff

surgery operation done by a doctor

Find Out More

NASA

www.nasa.gov/audience/forstudents/k-4/index.html
Find out more about aircraft and what astronauts do on this Website.

Science Games

pbskids.org/games/science.html
This PBS Website has a collection of science games that you can try.

Science Kids

www.sciencekids.co.nz
Learn more about the different sides of science by exploring this Website.

Science News

www.sciencenewsforkids.org
Learn what's new in the wide world of science by reading this Website.

Index